Petting Gilbert

by Michèle Dufresne

Pioneer Valley Educational Press, Inc

Kenny lived next door to Gilbert the pig and the farmer. Every day after school, Kenny visited Gilbert and all of the other animals on the farm.

Kenny liked to help the farmer take care of the animals. Sometimes he helped her clean the barn, and he helped her feed all of the animals.

Kenny fed the horse hay and apples. He fed the donkey corn, and he fed Gilbert his special diet food.

The horse and the donkey liked to be petted. Kenny petted them every day. Gilbert didn't like to be petted. Kenny would try to pet Gilbert, but Gilbert would just run away.

Kenny was sad.
"Gilbert won't let me pet him,"
he told the farmer.

"Gilbert doesn't like to be petted,
but he loves to be scratched,"
said the farmer.
"Find a sharp and pointed stick
and scratch Gilbert's back
with it."

Kenny found a sharp and pointed stick to scratch Gilbert with.
The farmer was right!
Gilbert loved to be scratched with the stick.
"Oink, oink! Oink, oink!"
said Gilbert when Kenny scratched him with the stick.

Now every day, after he fed
and petted all of
the other animals, Kenny would sit
and scratch Gilbert
with his sharp and pointed stick.
Gilbert was a happy pig.
"Oink, oink," said Gilbert.
"Oink, oink!"